W9-BWU-432

Goats

Julie Murray

Abdo
FARM ANIMALS
Kids

abdopublishing.com

Published by Abdo Kids, a division of ABDO, PO Box 398166, Minneapolis, Minnesota 55439.
Copyright © 2016 by Abdo Consulting Group, Inc. International copyrights reserved in all countries.
No part of this book may be reproduced in any form without written permission from the publisher.

Printed in the United States of America, North Mankato, Minnesota.

052015

092015

 THIS BOOK CONTAINS
RECYCLED MATERIALS

Photo Credits: iStock, Shutterstock

Production Contributors: Teddy Borth, Jennie Forsberg, Grace Hansen

Design Contributors: Candice Keimig, Dorothy Toth

Library of Congress Control Number: 2014960329

Cataloging-in-Publication Data

Murray, Julie.

 Goats / Julie Murray.

   p. cm. -- (Farm animals)

ISBN 978-1-62970-940-6

Includes index.

1. Goats--Juvenile literature.   I. Title.

636.3--dc23

                    2014960329

Table of Contents

Goats

Goats live on a farm.

4

Most goats are black, brown, or white. Some have spots or **markings**.

Goats have **horns**.

They also have a beard.

Girl goats are called nannies.
Boys are billy goats. Babies
are kids.

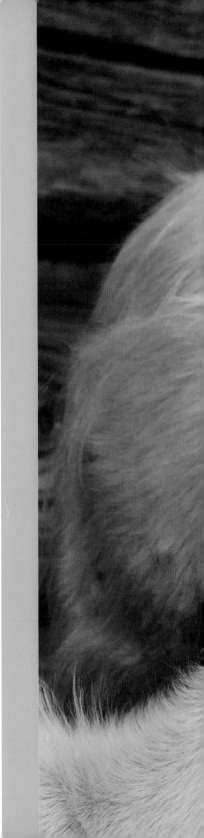

Goats say, "bleat."

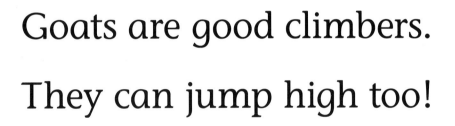

Goats are good climbers.

They can jump high too!

14

Goats eat leaves and grass.

They also eat **grain**.

People drink goat's milk.

It is also used to make cheese.

Have you seen goats on a farm?

20

A Goat's Life

climb things

get milked

eat

rest

Glossary

grain
the seeds of plants that are used for food.

horn
one of the hard pointed parts that grows on the head of some animals.

marking
a mark or repeated mark on an animal's fur or skin.

Index

abdokids.com

Use this code to log on to abdokids.com and access crafts, games, videos, and more!

Abdo Kids Code:
FGK9406